105 Body Resets

How the Body Lives Longer By Resetting 105 Critical Functions All The Time

David Gomadza

www.twofuture.world

PAPERBACK ISBN: 9798323489039

PAPERBACK ISBN: **9798323489039**

DEDICATION

To a better future.

CONTENTS

NB some of the text in this book looks and sounds alien but it's because it's brain language text and these are Wearable Brain Books meaning that the text should be as the text is in here but any other queries get in touch email us info@twofuture.world or davidgomadza@hotmail.com

00447719210295

ACKNOWLEDGMENTS

Tomorrow's World Order

105 CRITICAL BODY FUNCTION RESETS

The body must reset after every activity so that it prepares itself to do the same task that means the body itself is a set of predefined tasks that must be completed so that the same task can be done over and over again this is the trick to living longer if all the resets are completed perfectly on time then the body will last longer
Now let's see the list of all reset switched in the body the body has 109 critical reset switches that must be reset for life to continue without any problems
Now let's write down the list
1 anus
2 vaginal
3 penal
4 voice
5 ears
6 nose
7 head
8 accords
9 Ave instead
10 veins
11 Ave instead chords
12 aveins chords minus
13 Ave instead chords plus
14 avein chords
15 avein chords base
16 avein chords than
17 avein znkots
18 avein zktsonts
19 avein zknotszts

20 avein zknotsts
21 avein zknotstnst
22 avein zknotzstzs
23 anotsz
24 anotsz chords
25 anotsz chords not
26 anotsz chords divide
27 anotsz chords ztisde
28 anotsz chords bititzdes
29 anotsz chords citidestz
30 anotsz chords diditezi
31 anotsz chords fifitezi
32 anotsz chords skitzxegh
33 anotsz chords titizeti
34 anotzs chords titonet
35 anotzs chords Viviane
36 anotzs chords zizitinez
37 anotzs binords
38 anotsz vanords
39 anotz xixinords
40 hands
41 legs
42 chest
43 stomach
45 veins
46 neck
47 joints
48 backspin
49 spine
50 lips
51 cheeks
52 neck vest
53 chest vest
54 leg vest
55 arm vest
56 joint vest
57 jaw
58 jaw vest
59 chin
60 chin vest
61 top lip

62 bottom lip
63 tongue
64 tongue top
65 tongue tip
66 tongue bottom
67 tongue edge
68 tongue Perimeter
69 tongue joist
70 neck vest
71 neck side
72 neck back
73 neck tight
74 neck guard
75 neck masse
76 chest belt
77 chest vest [2]
78 chest tight 1
79 shoulder
80 shoulder collar bone
81 shoulder plate
82 shoulder guard
83 shoulder masse
84 shoulder side
85 shoulder fifi
86 shoulder arm
87 shoulder rest
88 shoulder back
89 shoulder musk
90 shoulder arm [2]
91 stomach cramp
92 stomach pain [2]
93 stomach ach
94 stomach belly configuration [after shitting]
95 sex
96 sex arm [after masturbation]
97 sex hast
98 sext vest
99 sex git
100 sex drum
101 sex drive
102 sex armchair

103 sex chain
104 shit chain
105 shit belt
Now that we have pointed to 105 needed resets we can also say these happen only as and when needed your body has what are reset switches that means after every activity the body lights up a switch indicating completed tasks that will need resetting just after they have occurred that means that whatever you do will need to be reset later on but most happen there and there automatically only 1 of the 105 switches occur at random this is the spine reset this is because this is needed to reset everything else that means without the spine reset then there is no other reset that can occur the only reason why spinal injuries affects the whole body all reset switches stops function meaning that all other activities will never happen again this is because to happen again they must first be reset to correct position
Now let's see the brain commands for all these ,[corresponds to 1 to 105 needed resets above]
1 start.anusreset.start
2 start.vaginareset.start
3 start.penalreset.start
4 start.voicereset.start
5 start.earsreset.start
6 start.nosereset.start
7 start.headreset.start
8 start.accordsreset.start
9 start.Aveinsteadreset.start [as if this is the first time because aveinstead rarely is reset]
10 start.veinsreset.start
11 start.Aveinsteadchordsreset.start
12 start.aveinschordsminusreset.start
13 start.Aveinsteadchordsplusreset.start
14 start.aveinchordsreset.start
15 start.aveinchordsbase.start
16 start.aveinchordsthan.start
17 start.aveinznkotsreset.start
18 start.aveinzktsontsreset.start
19 start.aveinzknotsztsreset.start
20 start.aveinzknotstsreset.start
21 start.aveinzknotstnstreset.start
22 start.aveinzknotzstzsreset.start
23 start.anotszreset.start

24 start.anotszchordsreset.start
25 start.anotszchordsnotreset.start
26 start.anotszchordsdividereset.start
27 start.anotszchordsztisdereset.start
28 start.anotszchordsbititzdesreset.start
29 start.anotszchordscitidestzreset.start
30 start.anotszchordsdiditezireset.start
31 start.anotszchordsfifitezireset.start
32 start.anotszchordsskitzxeghreset.start
33 start anotszchordstitizetireset.start
34 start.anotzschordstitonetreset.start
35 start.anotzs lchordsVivianereset.start
36 start.anotzschordszizitinezreset.start
37 start.anotzsbinordsreset.start
38 start.anotszvanordsreset.start
39 start.anotzxixinordsreset.start
40 start.handsreset.start
41 start.legsreset.start
42 start.chestreset.start
43 start.stomachreset.start
45 start.veinsreset.start
46 start.neckreset.start
47 start.jointsreset.start
48 start.backspinreset.start
49 start.spinereset.start
50 start.lipsreset.start
51 start.cheeksreset.start
52 start.neckvestreset.start
53 start.chestvestreset.start
54 start.legvestreset.start
55 start.armvestreset.start
56 start.jointvestreset.start
57 start.jawreset.start
58 start.jawvestreset.start
59 start.chinreset.start
60 start.chinvestreset.start
61 start.toplipreset.start
62 start.bottomlipreset.start
63 start.tonguereset.start
64 start.tonguetopreset.start
65 start.tonguetipreset.start

66 start.tonguebottomreset.start
67 start.tongueedgereset.start
68 start.tonguePerimeterreset.start
69 start.tonguejoistreset.start
70 start.neckvestreset.start
71 start.necksidereset.start
72 start.neckbackreset.start
73 start.necktightreset.start
74 start.neckguardreset.start
75 start.neckmassereset.start
76 start.chestbeltreset.start
77 start.chestvest[2]reset.start
78 start.chesttight1reset.start
79 start.shoulderreset.start
80 start.shouldercollarbonereset.start
81 start.shoulderplatereset.start
82 start.shoulderguardreset.start
83 start.shouldermassereset.start
84 start.shouldersidereset.start
85 start.shoulderfifireset.start
86 start.shoulderarmreset.start
87 start.shoulderrestreset.start
88 start.shoulderbackreset.start
89 start.shouldermuskreset.start
90 start.shoulderarm[2]reset.start
91 start.stomachcrampreset.start
92 start.stomachpain[2]reset.start
93 start.stomachachreset.start
94 start.stomachbellyconfiguration[after shitting]reset.start
95 start.sexreset.start
96 start.sexarm[after masturbation]reset.start
97 start.sexhastreset.start
98 start.sextvestreset.start
99 start.sexgitreset.start
100 start.sexdrumreset.start
101 start.sexdrivereset.start
102 start.sexarmchairreset.start
103 start.sexchainreset.start
104 start.shitchainreset.start
105 start.shitbeltreset.start
Now what we see is that everything we do in life at one point or the

other will need to be reset this is what improves human life than other lives some animals reset after every activity but we have the most reset in humans if we look at animals that live longer than humans like the tortoise or the guava all these animals have double the reset switches to humans does that mean the more resets the longer the life?

Now let's look at examples in play resets are done for things that can be carried out again unless if there is a reset life is possible because of resets if there were no resets the body would simply lose some functions or wear off over time of use the creator realized that the best way to self preservation is reset that means after every action the body must reset everything and this reset makes us who we are alive that means there is a correlation between life and reset the more resets happen the longer a person lives the body over time has realized this and now keeps a record of how many resets are needed for certain age to be reached and here is a list

Age 10 at least 1780 resets

Age 15 at least 2890 resets

Age 20 at least 8890 resets

Age 35 at least 90000 resets

Age 45 at least 170000 resets

Age 55 at least 280000 resets

Age 65 at least 740000 resets

Age 75 at least 890000 resets

Age 85 at least 900000 resets

Age 95 at least 910000 resets

Age 105 at least 111000000 resets

Now if we Ask a lot of questions then these are the questions

If we Ask what can be done this is the answer we can increase the rate of resets to increase the number over years what can be this is the answer we can reduce intervals between activity and reset what could be this is the answer we could also add alternatives to resets some functions can benefit if they use activities that offer the same without resets and these are

Smoking for sex

Wanking for sex

Mediate for eating

Talk for eating

Relax for straight binge eating

Ask for relaxation

View for acting

Acting for viewing but with limitations

Ask and get
Get to ask
Mint to fetch
Fetch to mint
Rewind to tone
Tone to rewind
Add to subtract
Subtract to add
Minus to add
Add to minus
Donate to ask
Ask to donate
Rejuvenate to rewind
Rewind to rejuvenate
If we Ask for everything our body recoil in advance so that when we
get it resets itself to neutral but if we get first it rebounces in
preparation for a recoil but if we keep asking your body is in constant
rebounce that means the reset will be cumbersome meaning you will
need to be asked as well to restore to neutral this is why the rich gives
but ask in kind
Now we can look at everything the body need resetting
The body must reset all these per day
1 anus even if you don't shit
2 vagina even if no sex
3 penis everyday even if you don't fuck
4 stomach even if you don't eat
5 liver even if you don't drink or eat
6 legs even if you don't walk
7 hands even if you don't touch or lift
8 head even if you don't use it
9 nose [sneeze] even if you don't sneeze
10 eyes [squint] even if you don't squint
11 hands [arms] even if you don't stretch your arms
12 armpits [rolls] even if you don't lift your hands
13 lips even if you don't lift your lips to talk or eat
14 tongue even is you don't eat or use it for talking
15 mouth even if you dont open it
Now lets ask a lot of related questions why we need everyday resets
critical functions must be reset on a daily basis used or not if not used
the reset will use it for that day and also perform the reset at the same
time what about the other resets when?

Now we look at period of reset or periods between resets if we Ask what can be done this is the answer we can always make room for something else that can make performance of a reset obvious we can easily add something on top so that even if we miss that activity reset is guaranteed and this is how we can do this

Add ask to everything and always says I ask for this this will make it easy for the body to perform the reset on a daily basis because you are actually telling it to perform even if the activity is not carried out that means we can talk to our bodies to carry on critical maintenance without the function occurring

Now if we Ask what could be this is the answer everything can be and is and will be the same forever this is the answer everything works perfectly and for thousand years has worked perfectly humans might not be able to live forever ceteris paribus but if they did I swear these resets would work forever as well the main reason is because these are predefined functions meaning will never make a mistake and as such will work forever

Now what could be this is the answer these functions need reset to prolong life image rebirth being reset over and over again

Now what can be done to further improve and increase their lifespan? We can add a lot of things like swapping one thing with the other but let the body do both resets this is clever in that the body shall keep resetting everything on a daily basis and the number of resets dictates how long the body is going to live if we Ask what could be then this is what could be the body can be made to reset by itself through brain commands but why this is not so is the fact that humans until now had not mastered what is needed to be Yahweh in order to understand the body first you must know the creator of the body then once you know how he thinks then you can know the body that means I am the only human being able to talk and ask the brain questions I know most people say it's the doctors but the brain hides from doctors find me a doctor who has ever communicated with the brain and the answer is nil in brain command answer no.doctor.talktobrain.human

That means on earth there is no single doctor who has ever communicated with the brain okay they attach neurons here to probe but that's just about it

Now let's look at critical functions that don't need reset but could benefit from a reset and how some functions like thinking can benefit from a reset the reason being that whenever we think a lot of movement occurs in the brain and a lot of heat is generated when we Ask what could be done then a reset point will make things better another function is eating when we eat then we must use a lot of stomach movements that can be done by an easy reset we can look at breathing but breathing must be continuous to sustain life that means only a reset just before death that would Kickstart everything

Now what could be with all these recommendations? The body can easily think and reset before the next thought we can eat and when we stop the body resets itself and we can live two lives because when we are about to die because of lack of oxygen the body can easily reset breathing to start again as at childbirth

Now let's look at other brain commands that can sum up this book

Ask.start.reset.me

WhenAskreset.start

Whatstart.me

Whatcanbe.ask

Whatcouldbe.start

Whatwas.start

Whatwasbutcouldbe.ask

Whatcanbe.ask

Whatwasbe.ask

Whenwas.ask

Whatif.ask

Whatcouldbe.ask

Now that we have highlighted the importance of reset in prolonging life we can conclude by asking a lot of questions

1 what was

2 what could be

3 what will be

4 what can be

5 what was but still could be

6 what is but could be

7 what has been and will be

8 what is and still is

9 what could be

10 what was

11 what will be

12 what is to be

13 what would be

14 what should be

15 what was but could be

16 what is but could not be

17 what is and is not

18 what could be but is not
19 what is and is not
20 what is but is not
21 what was but is not
22 what is but is not
23 what could be but is not
24 what is to be but can't be
25 what is to be but will not be
26 what is to be but can't be but
27 what is to be but could be but when
28 what is to be but might not be but could still be
29 what can be but is not but might be
30 what is and is not but can be
31 what was but is not but could still be
32 what will be but is not to be
33 what should be but is not
34 what could be but
35 what can be but when
36 what is but is not
37 what is but is not
38 what could be but is
39 what would be but is now
40 what is but when and how
41 what can be but is not
42 what is but is not to be
43 what if but
44 what can be but is not
45 what is but is but might not be
46 what is and when
47 when and what is to be
48 what is but is not
49 what can be but is
50 what was but might still be
The end.

ABOUT DAVID GOMADZA

Visit www.twofuture.world

Read the best book series;

Thoughts To Word or Audio

Visit

www.twofuture.world

We decoded God Yahweh and everything to do with life

Read our books to find out more

no.doctor.talktobrain.human

That means on earth there is no single doctor who has ever communicated with the brain okay they attach neurons here to probe but that's just about it

Only me has talked to the brain and can get all the answers we want

18